This book belongs to:

_____

Published by Penguin Books India
11 Community Centre, Panchsheel Park, New Delhi 110017

© PENGUIN BOOKS INDIA 2006

1 3 5 7 9 10 8 6 4 2

Printed at Ajanta Offset & Packagings Ltd, New Delhi

Life in the Forest

written by Vivek Menon
illustrated by Sanjay Sarkar

A forest is a place with lots of trees, bushes and grass. Many wild animals and birds live in the forest.

There are many kinds of
forests in the world.

pine forest

oak forest

rainforest

bush

jungle

scrub

There are many kinds of
creatures in a forest.
Some live in trees.
Some live in the bushes.
Some live on the ground.
Some live underground.

snake

termite

monkey

frog

9

This is the forest floor.

mole

anthill

beetle

mushroom

rat

13

Some animals in the forest eat grass.
Some animals eat leaves.
Some animals eat other animals.

zebra

elephant

giraffe

lion

15

Some animals and birds
in the forest live in trees
and shrubs.

squirrel

grasshopper

caterpillar

16

Some animals and birds live in the top of trees.

butterfly

tree frog

macaw

colobus

19

A forest is very useful for all the creatures that live in it. It is useful for people, too.

trees make the
air pure

trees are a home for
birds and animals

21

Forests are being
destroyed by people.
People cut down trees,
and kill animals and birds.

Forests grow with the help
of animals, birds and
insects.
People cannot grow forests.

tiger

peacock

crocodile

Did you spot these plants and trees in the forest?

Did you spot these creatures in the forest?

Index